Bird me
by Edith Azam

Translated from the French
and introduced by **Stuart Bell**

Published 2021 by the87press
The 87 Press LTD
87 Stonecot Hill
Sutton
Surrey
SM3 9HJ
www.the87press.com

First published as 'Oiseau-moi' by Les Éditions Lanskine
© Lanskine, Courcoué-sur-Logne, 2017
© Edith Azam, 2017
English translation © Stuart Bell, 2021

The moral right of Bird me has been asserted in accordance with the Copyright, Designs and Patents Act 1988

ISBN: 978-1-8380698-4-1

Cover photograph© Francesco Rossi, 2021
Design: Stanislava Stoilova [www.sdesign.graphics]

STUART BELL is a literary translator. His previous translations include the novels *They Stole Our Beauty* (2019) and *The Softest Sleep* (2020). He is currently editing a collection of essays for the87press on the moving power of artworks, forthcoming in 2021.

Introduction

I had the good fortune, while translating this collection, to be in email correspondence with Edith Azam. In her messages, always warm and unassuming, she spoke of how she sometimes disappears from the everyday world for lengthy periods, wandering into the mountains 'far from everything', to be with nature, to find oxygen. Through language, I could feel Azam's profound sense of connection to the Earth, to the sounds of the forest, to birdsong. Each one a beautiful poem of a kind, these emails allowed me to see that the act of writing is, for her, a process of writing from the ground upwards: a sensory channelling of nature's many modes. Such is the organic truth of Azam's work, she is well-known in contemporary French poetry circles for her aversion to self-capture in biography, as well as the more commercial trappings of the circuit. For Azam, listing her extensive catalogue of publications means framing her own personal history, and her writing, in a way that detracts from the authenticity and integrity of both. Our correspondence over this past year has opened my eyes to the value of seeing Azam, and this collection, as unclassifiable and unlistable. I have come to look upon *Bird me* as an event unto itself, as free-standing, a visceral memory of long hours spent self-searching beside the river, each poem a ribboning interruption on its surface.

Enamoured of Azam's sensitivity as I translated, I found myself resisting contextualisation of this work within the wider landscape of contemporary French literature. To read this collection most headily and most truly, it may be more important to open oneself up to the immediate simplicity of its objects and places as discoveries, to the purity of its exploration of language. The twenty-seven untitled poems in *Bird me* turn upon four recurring symbols, timeless images akin to those found in a dream state: pebbles, a river, a chestnut tree, and a bird. This final image, the most central to the collection, is one which haunts and inspires the poetic voice. This voice may or may not be Azam herself, or else a hybrid, lyrical 'I', as unfixed as the haunting bird of the collection's title. This bird, referred to as 'Hannah', is addressed in each poem. The eponymous palindrome takes on different rôles and guises: there are moments in which Hannah is celebrated as muse, love object, mediator between the poet body and the natural world; at other times, she is an all-consuming force, deadly and destructive to a point where the poetic voice is afraid even to say her name out loud.

'Who, or what, is Hannah?' may be the question at the heart of this collection. It is also the question addressed in the first poem's opening line: '*Hannah is a bird / Hannah is… / Hannah I'd love / to be her nest*'. If identity and desire are laid bare at the offset, the ensuing narrative goes on to explore, and to problematise, the apparent certainty of this opening. Hannah is a bird, yet she may also incarnate the act of writing poetry, the complexity of links between the poetic mind and the world around her. Hannah is both longed for: '*It was on the riverbank / and I wanted you to kiss me*' and endured: '*Hannah rubs me out / Hannah puts a knife in my heart*'. Hannah seems both to suffer: '*I've got my bird in tears / hiccupping ill*' and to cause suffering: '*In a single day Hannah / strips my body / wrings out / its vocabulary*'. The poetic voice is bewitched by her, indebted to her, and yet too is appalled and tormented by her lacerating force. Interrupting this relay between love and pain are the recurring symbols of the river, pebbles, and chestnut tree. These act as temporary defences, as sites of refuge, from Hannah and the starkness of her horror-jouissance. While the river is a sealed-off mass of secrets with pebbles skimming across its surface, the chestnut tree is a private symbol of swelling love for Hannah, internalised and guarded so that Hannah cannot desecrate it: '*For her I planted / a chestnut tree in my mind / one of the biggest / for a thousand winters*'. The poetic 'I' appears fully aware of the havoc that Hannah can wreak: '*You're my danger*', and yet she remains unchangingly a medium for capturing human experience in writing: '*And you're my poetry*'. This leads to a memorable dream-like moment in which the 'I' comes across a hundred benches and abandons her torn-up draft pages in order to write anew: '*I engrave / write loving words / and bird flight*'.

Yet while it may seem that the punishing avian muse leaves the poetic voice entirely powerless, the voice finds resources in language, perhaps fuelled by Hannah's longed-for menace, in order to capture and subvert in writing the one who holds her in rapture. One example is the abandonment of French, replaced by words and short phrases borrowed from English, Italian, and Spanish in order to admonish or praise Hannah in a tongue which may not necessarily be understandable to her. Drawing from Italian, she calls Hannah her '*uccellina*', 'little bird' in the feminine form. This recalls closely the verb 'uccellare', meaning 'to catch birds', as well as 'to fool' or 'to trick': a keen reminder of the arresting and reductive power of the poet's polyglot plume. Another resource is the skilful and playful subversion of spelling and grammar, designed perhaps to destabilise Hannah, or to rewrite her from within, inside the economy of the carnage-bliss that is her world. The 'I' lovingly mocks Hannah in English by referring to her as her '*mokingbird*', the letter 'c' omitted in an attempt to reassert control via the creation of her own hybrid language. Elsewhere, evoking her fear that Hannah may forget her, the poetic voice offers up the image of the forget-me-not flower, '*myosotis*' in French, except here she rewrites the flower at the intersection between French and

English, claiming Hannah as her own by splitting '*myosotis*' into '*My Osotis*'. Crowned by this newfound upper-case 'O', Hannah is temporarily harnessed within the '*my*' possessive, her wings clipped in words.

The *Bird me* poems read most hypnotically when spoken aloud. Colons hold up moments of inner finding, while recurring rows of dots allow thoughts to trail off and break away, as if taking flight themselves. These circles in punctuation may be seen as captures in print of the rings the 'I' finds all around her: in bird flight in the sky, in the holes in her own skin made by Hannah's pecking beak, and in the tidal waters of the Seine where the titanic Hannah sinks a boat. Moving through the untitled yet clearly demarcated verses, seasons come and go, both realised and imagined, from: '*It's snowing her voice in my head*' to: '*Hoops are turning / from snow and sun / and burn me*'. Time passes, from sleepless nights spent in an icy bedroom to hours wiled away on the tree-lined riverbank, the rituals of thinking and writing bringing agony and ecstasy, culminating in a conclusion of sorts which each reader, or listener, can interpret for themselves.

Gathered collectively the verses seem to expand, both on the page during reading and in wider memory, akin to the imagined chestnut tree which starts to outgrow the space in which it was planted. There is no French rhyme scheme to be preserved in translation, and departures from the original are very few. Sections in Italian and Spanish I have left untranslated, while those parts originally in English I have bracketed in order to simulate a sense of distance and removal, as I imagine non-anglophone audiences may experience it. The original title *Oiseau–moi* I have translated into English without the hyphen, owing to my interpretation of this as an imperative, or command form, most usually hyphenated in French, yet not in English. *Bird me* as title is inspired by the lines: '*Mange–moi*' ('*Eat me*') and: '*Arrache–moi*' ('*Pull from me*') understood as commands; although not entirely unambiguous, this title speaks to the experience of being 'birded', of psychically receiving and feeling Hannah in all her potent majesty, of summoning her to unleash her full powers, conjuring the one within the natural world who makes metamorphosis possible, a devastating and unforgiving love that births poetry.

This translation is the result of an incredibly special collaboration between the highly inclusive and progressive publication houses The 87 Press (UK) and Les Éditions Lanskine (France). Following the United Kingdom's 2016 announcement to break with the European Union, and at a point in time when intereuropean relations appear more tenuous and fractured than ever, it is hoped that this translation may play a small part, however tremulous, in carrying creative voices across borders. I would like to thank Edith Azam, Azad Ashim Sharma, and Kashif Sharma-Patel for their candour and support in the realisation of this project.

Stuart Bell

Hannah is a bird
Hannah is…
Hannah I'd love
to be her nest.
Tall trees line the Seine
and by the water
I while away the time
waiting for her to remember
(don't forget me
forget me not and…)
But Hannah couldn't care less no doubt
and there's little doubt
she doesn't care.
Hannah is my bird
and all the while
nailed to the ground
I flap my arms
to shed this scarecrow's wings :
my carcass.

What keeps me silent ?
If you knew
if you knew Hannah
the heavy plaque
a bird lifts
flying across open sky.
And so eyes lowered
I dive
into the Seine
imagining that one day...
Imagining that one day
all that I imagine...

Hannah
my hands are restless
and it's coursing through me :
the fracture.
I'm afraid so afraid
how I'm shaking…
I hear
a cracking
contaminate :
my language.
Sleepless nights
I go from one
to the next
head tipped back.
Words cascading everywhere
always the bones that creak.
The gap is widening
inescapable…
My open body
has no room
the air is coarse
I am halved
and surprised once again
when I realise :
that I exist.
Loving justifies this :
and adjusts me.

It's snowing.
It's snowing her voice in my head
and I close my ears
to block out anything else.
Slowly flakes
cover the Seine.
Behind me
no trace
no one will know
I passed by
the tide rises
my mind's own falls
Hannah will know nothing
of the bird that she makes me.

Hannah rubs me out Hannah puts
a knife in my heart
wind in my lungs
a flash on my shoulder
little besos
stolen from Norge.
Inside
monkey leaps
cling–fall all alone
from one illusion to the next.
In a single day Hannah
strips my body
wrings out :
the vocabulary
and it makes me shake.
For her I planted
a chestnut tree in my mind
one of the biggest
for a thousand winters
and so that she might have
roots...
Hannah Hannah,
My Osotis,
(Don't forget me
Don't forget...)
I won't be able to
No I won't be able :
to switch myself off...

Hannah plays at deception
she cheats my nights :
what can I say ?
I awaken all the jolts
each time I hear her voice.
Playful Hannah is playing me
(you're my danger Hannah...)
Yet mute she stays
chooses all her silences
while mine gather
in my throat.
Hence the absolute necessity
of writing this poem
of being able at last to say her name
less fearful :
of using it.
Yes I know very well
all this all this
is always
language
a question
of death.
How to stay on track?
What does it matter
I don't give a damn
Because the life that I have lost
And then this other :
that I now have to lose...
Not any old how nor
for any old thing...

Hannah
I would like to tell her that...
I would like to tell her
that I would like to no longer wait
yet I will go on waiting for her
I will wait patiently up to the end
and up to the trees
to the birds.
Let the birds
devour me Hannah
the birds...
So make the most
of it because afterwards
my language :
will be screwed.

I look at my hands
dream up a river for each.
I dream up rivers
and then ?
Nothing.
Under the bridge
is all my love on the lookout
reflections on the water yet...
under the bridge there is :
nothing.
I put the rivers back
in my pockets
and the great chestnut tree
ruffles my mind...
I walk I walk
telling stories.
One day
tomorrow
one day
before
yesterday
whenever
it was on the riverbank
and I wanted you to kiss me.
When you kiss me,...
If you kiss me Hannah you will see I...

an a–grammatical silence
empties my lungs
Hannah Hannah
if you knew…
If you knew
all the birdness
I kiss them
all the while thinking
about kissing you.
(Hannah my Dear
You're my absence…)

Hannah I wrote
everywhere in the middle of the bedroom
on all the walls of memory
and in the eddies of the Seine
I clenched my fists I dived
then wrote Hannah.
I wrote it for a very very long time
I wrote slowly
each letter responding
to its counterpart
front to back
in any direction
the name Hannah
my oxy–love
patience
desire.
Hannah Hannah
my Osotis
my mokingbird
beso beso
Osotis mine
otro beso
ma Segnorita :
Uccellina !

I throw a pebble on the Seine
and the birds zigzag
and the birds streak me.
Circles swirl and merge
I murmur your name
walk underwater Hannah
in hardly–formed thoughts.
Eat me
Eat me Uccellina
for it's you I'm thinking of
and these sensations I create
it's to you I owe them.
Hannah Hannah
beauty bird,
we all have our own unique
fiction.
Living
what of it ?
A decir ?
Hannah we are wind
charred creations...
A signed forehead
language stitched...
(You're my danger
Hannah
and you're...
my poetry).

There are hundreds of benches
and here again I engrave
write loving words
and bird flight.
I am
I know
she doesn't know :
I resist
telling myself
that Hannah is there
because quite simply :
she is.
Doesn't stand to reason ?
No matter
I dream of uncanny confusion
beyond all expression.
No meaning no meaning
I'm afraid Hannah...
I swallow a little of the night
to calm myself
black pebble iced circles
it's so sad so...
It would be good if sometimes
tiredness would rest.
It would be good :
to diminish...
No meaning no meaning...

I touch my bones :
they are growing back.
My body lives in other places.
No meaning I'm cold
afraid of being cold.
I've got my bird in tears
hiccupping ill
from May right up to the North Pole.
Hannah Hannah
I put words to sentences
with no outline left
no no Hannah
no not that
not like that.

Sometimes Hannah
the clouds in the water
look like my brain.
Pit–a–pat
I throw a pebble :
breaks in two.
All around me
hoops are turning
from snow and sun
and burn me.
Good grief Hannah
this delicacy is it you ?
And that terrible beso…
All this
my two arms unfolding
make my body
a little less
ill.
Your beak pecking in my agony
if you knew
if you knew Hannah
how it runs through
and redimensions me :
in space.
And in the place
where I create myself
there is nothing to flee
I am totally :
off–topic.

Hannah you know
with the chestnut tree
outgrowing my skull
sometimes I no longer know
where my bones went
falling from the tree :
or me.
White pebble blue circles
What reader
will follow you
today ?
What time is it ?
In which syntax ?
I swap circles
write a letter to you
write to you then tear it up
May I send them to you :
the shreds ?

I draw up a list in my head
I count the pebbles
I want to decode
everything
tease from the number
a non–being...
Hannah I don't want her
she is enjoying herself
being :
a number.
She doesn't care :
perfect !
Let her sing
her own tune
because that's what
birds do.
My feet on the waterline
I find a long silence
that I fight for
then against
proving fatal :
writing inside.
A few commas on the water
stitch my shadow
with lined spaces
through which I see her pass.
Knives scissors
forks in the depths
all this because a bird
is dismantling my head
chirping in my mind.

To tell Hannah
I would like her to know too :
I dream wide
through my shredded nights
talking to myself in the chaos
I dream
carnage.
I go into the streets
barefoot I listen mechanical
to the clocks
and feel myself suddenly aging.

I dream Hannah
I dream to the point
of breathlessness
face to face before the night
aiming yet
verging on
tentative
misery–maker :
I dream Hannah
I dream
and sleep peels away
currents break me apart
confined I hold my breath
my hands turn to flippers
digging the watery depths.

Hannah every day
I wake up
and am no longer sure
is it her or me :
speaking.
In the bedroom winter
hangs at the windows
the curtains have frozen
and words erase themselves
to the sounds of bones.
Walls split
and my head...
I look into the void
throw a pebble
they fascinate me
all those circles :
how so much emptiness
can be filled by a nothing.
There is so much to say...
There is so much to say
that words
words no longer mean anything
no longer fleshy
when I say them.
Need to find myself
another :
language
to think up by hand.
I step into the void
listen to the birds
look at all the solitude.

Hannah is a bird
the bird circles deafeningly.
Of course it doesn't matter.
I am a chestnut tree
my head is a pebble
my pebble a stream
my head is…
in my pockets.
(Why?
Why not?)
My head knits words
Unknits them straightaway
My head throws pebbles
to make its own :
vocabulary.

I vocabubble
blue circles
that take off without me
taking off or not
on the Seine.
The chestnut tree
ruffles me
unfolds me in circles
in–the–water–in–the–air
a nothing.
Then a skipping stone
lands at my throat
and suddenly :
total silence.
My scar
opens once again.
I place a pebble
on my skull
the bird approaches
then eats it
leaving unknown words
to restitch
my mind
just a little.

Along the quayside
this time a boat.
I watch it sail away
thinking Hannah might come
the boat sways
it really wouldn't take much
sways a lot
for her to…
Too late :
sunk.
Another boat in my hands
I set it down on the water.
To the currents
I add a little sky
dip a pebble
a beso ?
I dip a beso :
into life.
The rings ?
It's Hannah who is drawing them
she's the one circling.
It's Hannah dancing
who makes the Seine dance.
They think it's me they are seeing :
but Hannah's the one there.

What does it mean
Hannah
does it mean
having a bird in your blood ?
Do you know how it feels
your flesh riddled with beak pecks ?
And these billions of holes
for these billions of missing things ?
Hannah mi huracan
mi tormenta :
disconocida !
Eres mi escándalo
y yo ti gusto :
escandalosamente !
Hannah I would like to tell her
tell her about life
long long ago
and that everything is screwed Hannah.
For the original circle :
un gran brasero.

Un tan grande brasero
for the dancefloor.
Tailored to the Seine
are the bones
it carries along.
You want to give yourself over again
to write all the better
because you can't
but there is nothing
nothing :
to be saved
not even
a beating of wings.

Strange stone
circle unparalleled
and in the sickly sky
birds draw lines
that no longer write anything.
What can be said about her life ?
The Seine knows more
about it than I do and...
Of course I'm afraid but...
Of course
I dive.
Looks as if I'm dying
Yes I accept it I'm dying
(perhaps another time)
because this is not death
(perhaps otros besos)
so much as welcoming death
Hannah my Osotis
and so–much–love Hannah.
Because the body
definitive
the body undresses us
and what will remain of it :
less than nothing.

Life Hannah :
is wailful
and this bird wails loudly
until my bones twist :
from the head.
My body
I see its factory
I see all those words
weighing down.
Pull from me
Pull from me Hannah
this earth language !
Bring me above ground a little
so that everything :
so that everything isn't for breaking
so that this race to the void :
exhausts me into a better.
Life ?
It is straw.
For making fire with
burning only for us
burning only us
and then ?
Only thank you Hannah
you pull the words from me
that none know how to live.

Sitting by the water's edge
I wait for all the birds
then the last bird and then
the last dog.
Yet I know very well
that here in the place I am
no one will come
I am too far away
much too far away.
Day's end
and the birds gather
mark the sky
with their wide flight
and stroke their scores
of cries.
Hannah I would like to tell her
I would like to tell her the birds
that it will never be the same again
never again will they be :
the same birds...
And that yes Hannah
I will hang on each day
because the birds are there
and because having written it
for you too
perhaps one day the birds...
the birds will be :
different.